E-Careers

Careers in
Info Tech

Pat Rarus

ReferencePoint
Press®

San Diego, CA

About the Author

Pat Rarus loves writing, especially about technology. She holds a bachelor of arts degree in journalism and a master of science degree in mass communications, both from San Diego State University. She has worked as a professional writer/editor for more than twenty years and lives in Oceanside, California.

For more information, contact:
ReferencePoint Press, Inc.
PO Box 27779
San Diego, CA 92198
www.ReferencePointPress.com

Picture Credits:

Cover: Dmytro Zinkevych/Shutterstock.com
 6: Maury Aaseng
13: Hiraman/iStock.com
39: gorodenkoff/iStock.com
46: NicoElNino/iStock.com
71: sturti/iStock.com

LIBRARY OF CONGRESS CATALOGING-IN-PUBLICATION DATA

Name: Rarus, Pat, author.
Title: Careers in Info Tech/by Pat Rarus.
Description: San Diego, CA: ReferencePoint Press, Inc., 2020. | Series: E-Careers series | Includes bibliographical references and index.
Identifiers: LCCN 2018053853 (print) | LCCN 2018054865 (ebook) | ISBN 9781682826140 (eBook) | ISBN 9781682826133 (hardback)
Subjects: LCSH: Information technology—Vocational guidance.
Classification: LCC T58.5 (ebook) | LCC T58.5 .R37 2020 (print) | DDC 004.023—dc23
LC record available at https://lccn.loc.gov/2018053853

Contents

An Exciting, Ever-Changing Industry

Most teens cannot imagine life without smartphones or social media sites like Snapchat and Instagram. Yet some students may not even realize that this technology, which many people now take for granted, has only been around for a little more than a decade. In 2007, when Apple chief executive officer Steve Jobs introduced the iPhone, it seemed like a technological revolution had taken place. Now this so-called tech revolution is creating an array of new career opportunities.

A Variety of Career Choices

The fact that technology is now a daily part of life is but one of the many reasons a career in information technology (IT) is so promising. Now and in the future, IT workers will have many professional choices available to them. "Demand for tech workers continues to grow at a pace that's unmatched in other industries," says Raj Mukherjee, a senior vice president with the job search website Indeed. "Several in-demand roles . . . will continue to attract heavy growth in the coming few years," he commented in a 2017 *ZDNet* blog post. These "in-demand roles" include computer technical support specialists, database administrators, website developers, mobile app developers, business intelligence analysts, cloud solutions architects, cybersecurity analysts, and IT consultants.

However, careers in this dynamic field will undergo change as often as technology does. Tim Herbert, a senior vice president at CompTIA, a technology trade association, says that those interested in working in IT should be prepared to evolve throughout their career. During a 2018 interview with tech writer Mary K. Prattil in *CIO* magazine, Herbert commented that "growth is projected for nearly every IT occupation we see now through 2026, but the roles are changing and evolving."

With so many changes and evolutions, how should a student decide which IT career to pursue? Start by taking classes in the most popular computer languages and honing skill sets with proven future demand. "Development skills will continue to be among the hottest skills in the coming decade," says Herbert. "Organizational IT departments will have a growing need for specific [coding] languages." He expects C++, Django, JavaScript, Python, R, Ruby, and Ruby on Rails to be among the important languages for IT professionals to know in the years ahead.

The Demand for Data-Related Skills

The 2017 *Quant Crunch* tech report predicts that the number of data-related jobs in the United States will grow significantly through 2024. These positions will require IT professionals to have a mix of skills, including strong mathematical ability, knowledge of cloud applications and computer languages, and strong communication and data analysis skills. This expertise will help IT workers work with three increasingly important components of information technology: analytics, machine learning, and artificial intelligence.

Analytics is the discovery, interpretation, and communication of meaningful patterns in data. Machine learning is a type of data analysis that uses algorithms that learn from data. Algorithms tell a computer precisely what steps to take to solve a problem or reach a goal. Artificial intelligence (AI) provides

Great Jobs in Info Tech

Occupation	Minimum Educational Requirement	2017 Median Pay
Computer hardware engineer	Bachelor's degree	$115,120
Computer network architect	Bachelor's degree	$104,650
Computer support specialist	Associate's degree	$52,810
Computer systems analyst	Bachelor's degree	$88,270
Electrical and electronics engineer	Bachelor's degree	$97,970
Forensic science technician	Bachelor's degree	$57,850
Information security analyst	Bachelor's degree	$95,510
Market research analyst	Bachelor's degree	$63,230
Multimedia artist and animator	Bachelor's degree	$70,530
Software developer	Bachelor's degree	$103,560
Web developer	High school diploma	$67,990

Source: Bureau of Labor Statistics, *Occupational Outlook Handbook*, 2019. www.bls.gov.

systems with the ability to learn without being explicitly programmed. This enables computers to find data within data without human intervention. AI makes it possible for machines to learn from experience, adjust to new inputs, and perform humanlike tasks. Data scientists, big data engineers, database managers and developers, and data architects all work with analytics, machine learning, and AI.

Scrambling for Cybersecurity Skills

Cybersecurity is the practice of protecting systems, networks, and programs from digital attacks. Such attacks intend to access, change, or destroy private information, such as Social Security numbers and account passwords. Attacks may also be intended to con users out of money by, say, impersonating a relative claiming to be in financial need. Developing foolproof cybersecurity measures is especially challenging because at present there are so many different devices and operating systems. Attackers are also learning to trick computer users in more elaborate and confusing ways.

Because of ever-increasing digital attacks, companies are actively looking for cybersecurity workers. "One of the most in-demand IT positions is cybersecurity, and that demand is expected to grow dramatically as the volume and complexity of systems increases—and as hackers become increasingly skilled," says Tom Bakker of the Chicago-based staffing firm LaSalle Network in a January 2018 interview posted on the *CIO* website. Demand already outpaces supply, Bakker adds, and that gap will only expand in the upcoming years. In fact, the Global Information Security Workforce Study, conducted every two years, predicts that there will be a shortage of 1.8 million cybersecurity professionals by 2022. This will leave organizations aggressively competing for experienced cybersecurity talent.

IT Use Is Expanding Across the Industry

Some students find the technology world's constant changes to be confusing, and they may be unsure what tech career might be right for them. However, this fast-paced industry will offer them a wide variety of professional choices when they graduate. Almost every industry uses information technology in some way, and this will continue to be true in the future. For example, the health care industry will have a growing need for IT workers as hospitals and medical offices expand their use of electronic records and telemedicine (which involves diagnosing medical conditions at home). The financial services industry is also expanding digitally. Increases in mobile banking and online investing will require IT workers to keep customer data safe and make electronic transactions quick and easy. As retailers broaden their online offerings, they will need more business intelligence analysts to interpret and use customer data. All of these possibilities make it a great time to pursue a career in information technology.

Computer Technical Support Specialist

When computer users have trouble logging on or setting up a router, they often turn to a computer technical support specialist for help. These dedicated technology experts work in corporate offices, universities, and call centers. Their main job is to accommodate the often-desperate requests for help. Their primary goal is to provide the necessary assistance in a friendly and effective manner. "We need to make sure we know how to diagnose their issues and do it quickly," said senior computer technical support specialist Guido Diaz in an interview with *U.S. News & World Report*.

These specialists troubleshoot and solve problems with a calm, focused demeanor and a can-do attitude. They draw on their general knowledge of computer systems, hardware, and software as well as their expertise with specific products, such as Microsoft's

At a Glance

Computer Technical Support Specialist

Minimum Educational Requirements
Associate's degree; bachelor's degree preferred

Personal Qualities
Critical-thinking and problem-solving abilities; strong active listening and speaking skills

Certification
Recommended

Working Conditions
Indoors

Salary Range
About $31,070 to $90,890

Number of Jobs
As of 2016, 835,300

Future Job Outlook
Growth rate of 11 percent through 2026

Office 2019 for Windows and Mac. Some individuals work for technical support service companies, but others work within corporations or agencies.

Their job duties include troubleshooting operating system and software malfunctions. Some computer technical support specialists may even need to pull out a screwdriver to open up a laptop to check the motherboard (main circuit board) to replace a blown fuse. Considering the number of tasks, phone calls, face-to-face meetings, e-mails, and conversations they engage in each day, people in this line of work must possess excellent communication skills. They need to ask users the right questions to pinpoint the issue, figure out a solution, and then guide someone else through the fix step-by-step.

One type of computer technical support specialist focuses on network-related issues. Referred to as computer network support specialists, these professionals receive their fair share of distressed phone calls and e-mails. However, these help requests often revolve around network problems and come from fellow employees at their workplace. Network support specialists troubleshoot an organization's system for potential problems and provide regular maintenance. Their job is to ensure that the system and all of its components function properly.

Diverse is probably the best way to describe the workday of most computer technical support specialists. On any given day, they help people who are experiencing a wide variety of technical glitches. Perhaps a hard drive is malfunctioning, or a user is having trouble accessing his or her account information. Other common complaints include printers that do not work, wireless networks that keep kicking users off their computers, or devices that do not seem to connect.

When they are not on the phone helping customers, computer technical support specialists test and evaluate existing network systems, including local area networks (LANs), wide area networks (WANs), and Internet systems. They also back up network files and perform maintenance tasks daily, weekly, or monthly; these are critical to an organization's disaster recovery plan. This plan is a documented procedure for protecting data in the event of a power outage (which would be considered a natural disaster) or a terrorist attack (known as a human-made disaster). Organizations cannot always avoid disasters, but with careful planning, specialists can help minimize computer downtime and data loss.

How Do You Become a Computer Technical Support Specialist?

Education

All employers require their computer technical support specialists to have computer expertise, but many are flexible regarding how employees come by it. Although some will only hire specialists with a bachelor's degree, this is not always the case. Other employers only require job candidates who have an associate's degree in computer science, and some might hire workers who have only taken some computer classes. Perhaps even more important than a formal degree is a candidate's familiarity with Windows and Mac operating systems and servers as well as Cisco, Apple, and Microsoft products.

Certification

Because certification demonstrates competence in the field, passing a certification test may improve a specialist's chances of finding a job. Many companies and associations offer certification. Individuals must pass an exam (or a series of them) to become certified. According to the job search website Simply Hired, Microsoft's certified desktop support specialist, CompTIA's A+ and Network+, and Microsoft technology associate IT certifications are the most popular for computer technical support specialists.

Internships

Many employers offer internships to college students who are pursuing a bachelor's degree in computer science, information technology, or a related field. An internship can last for ten to twelve weeks or take place throughout the entire year. Interns must know how to troubleshoot problems that commonly crop up on both Mac and Windows platforms. Many internships are paid, ranging from about fifteen dollars an hour up to about twenty-four dollars an hour, with the possibility of thirty-five dollars an hour for overtime work. In addition, some companies offer interns bonuses of up to $4,800, according to the career website PayScale.

Some students participate in unpaid internships in exchange for college credit; such experiences can offer interns the chance to be mentored by knowledgeable experts in the field. Mentorships can teach students vital technical skills as well as soft skills, such as tact and diplomacy, which are usually needed when interacting with customers. Still other internships may lead to full-time, permanent employment. Because mentorships and on-the-job training are so important to aspiring computer technical support specialists, any type of internship—whether paid or unpaid—is a good idea.

Skills and Personality

Aspiring computer technical support specialists must understand log-in systems, e-mail applications, and network logistics. They must also enjoy troubleshooting. Fixing computer problems over the phone requires a specialist to mentally take apart a computer or imagine a customer's network setup without actually seeing it. The next step is to explain the problem to the person on the other end of the call. While the problem may be obvious to the specialist, the customer may lack experience with computers. Therefore, specialists need excellent communication skills. The job involves not only figuring out how to solve problems but also determining what caused the problems in the first place. To do this, a specialist must conduct very clear, direct conversations with clients. Indeed, a big part of the job is asking very specific, targeted questions to find out what is wrong.

Strong writing skills are also important; computer technical support specialists must write summaries of daily troubleshooting activities or submit monthly or quarterly reports to management.

Tech support specialists assist customers who are experiencing difficulties online. Troubleshooting problems is a big part of this job.

Part of their job might also include writing software, network, or other types of computer-related user manuals for customers and employees.

These specialists should also be able to juggle several issues at a time and be ready to tackle the various—and sometimes unexpected—problems that might cross their desks. This requires a cool, calm demeanor and the ability to handle stress—or at least conceal it when interacting with customers, coworkers, and supervisors. Computer technical support specialist jobs are a good fit for extroverted individuals who exude patience and are good at giving clear, concise instructions. "As long as you enjoy troubleshooting and talking to people and know what you're doing, you'll like this job," says Diaz.

Employers

Computer technical support specialists work for a wide variety of organizations, including Fortune 500 companies like Amazon, Apple, Microsoft, Google, and Oracle. They also work for government agencies, government contractors, hospitals, colleges and universities, large financial institutions, insurance companies, telecommunications firms, aerospace companies, and start-ups. Once hired, specialists usually receive on-the-job training that lasts from a week to a year. Many receive training throughout their careers to keep up with the fast-paced changes that define the industry.

Working Conditions

Computer technical support specialists work indoors and spend long hours in front of a computer. If they provide help-desk support, they spend many hours on the phone assisting callers with requests for technology services, repair or support requests, complaints, and inquiries.

Specialists usually work full-time. However, many do not work typical office hours of 8:00 a.m. to 5:00 p.m. Because computer support is vital for businesses, support is often required twenty-four hours a day. Some of this support may be performed remotely, but many specialists must still be available to work nights, weekends, or holidays.

Earnings

The Bureau of Labor Statistics (BLS) reports that in 2017 computer technical support specialists earned a median salary of $52,810. The highest-paid 10 percent in the profession earned $90,890 that year, and the lowest-paid 10 percent earned $31,070. The highest-paid specialists work in the metropolitan area of San Jose, San Francisco, and San Rafael, in California. The Fairbanks, Alaska, area also pays well, as does the city of

Lowell, Massachusetts, where many technology companies are located.

Opportunities for Advancement

Advancement for computer technical support specialists may mean handling more complex problems and products. Assuming these additional responsibilities will likely result in a higher salary or even a change in job title. Specialists often advance into management roles or get promoted to other IT positions, such as database administrator, software engineer, or computer programmer.

What Is the Future Outlook for Computer Technical Support Specialists?

According to the BLS, employment in this field is projected to grow 11 percent through 2026, which is faster than the average for all occupations. As organizations upgrade their outdated hardware, software, and network equipment and require experienced, knowledgeable professionals to field computer-related questions, computer technical support specialists will remain in demand, according to the *U.S. News & World Report Best Jobs* publication in 2017. Additional job growth will come from specific industries that rely heavily on technology, such as the software publishing industry as well as the management, scientific, and technical consulting industries.

Health care is one area that is expected to experience higher demand for IT support services. The health care industry increasingly requires technology to diagnose health problems, reduce medical errors, provide safer care at lower costs, and track and store patient data. However, such data must be shared across a variety of platforms, and it must be kept secure. Advanced IT support makes it possible for health care providers to better manage patient care while securing very sensitive data.

Association of Support Professionals (ASP)
500 Rincon de Romos SE
Rio Rancho, NM 87124
website: https://asponline.com

The ASP is an international membership organization for customer support managers and professionals. In addition to its annual Ten Best Web Support Sites awards, the ASP publishes research reports on a wide range of support topics, including support compensation, fee-based support, and services marketing. The ASP also provides its members with discounts and career development services.

Help Desk Institute (HDI)
21 S. Tejon St., Suite 1100
Colorado Springs, CO 80903
website: www.thinkhdi.com

For more than thirty years, the HDI has partnered with thousands of organizations to improve their customer service and service management performance by providing education and support. Through events, certification and training, consulting, membership, and industry resources, the HDI aims to transform service and support organizations and reimagine their approach to delivering exceptional service and value.

IEEE Computer Society
10662 Los Vaqueros Cir.
Los Alamitos, CA 90720-1314
website: www.computer.org

Part of the Institute of Electrical and Electronics Engineers, the IEEE Computer Society is the world's leading membership organization dedicated to computer science and technology. Serving more than sixty thousand members, the society is a trusted source for information, networking, and career development.

It serves a global community of technology leaders, including researchers, educators, software engineers, IT professionals (including computer technical support specialists), employers, and students. The organization sponsors more than two hundred technical conferences and events each year, including the industry-oriented Rock Stars series.

National Center for Women & Information Technology

University of Colorado
Campus Box 417 UCB
Boulder, CO 80309
website: www.ncwit.org

The National Center for Women & Information Technology is the only national nonprofit focused on women's participation in computing. It helps more than eleven hundred organizations recruit, retain, and advance women who pursue degrees in information technology and work in the industry.

Network Professional Association (NPA)

3517 Camino del Rio South, Suite 215
San Diego, CA 92108-4098
website: www.npanet.org

The NPA is a self-regulating, nonprofit association of network computing professionals, including computer technical support specialists, that sets standards of technical expertise and professionalism. Members participate in various boards, local chapters, committees, and councils. The NPA also offers membership to students who are enrolled in information technology classes at accredited colleges.

Database Administrator

Database administrators (DBAs) are the gatekeepers of electronic data. They use computers and software to keep data safe, organized, and properly stored. DBAs make sure that only authorized users can see and use the data. They have the vital responsibility of keeping their organization's database active and intact, protecting it from would-be hackers—in other words, keeping out the bad guys. Indeed, with information now so readily available through mobile devices, apps, tablets, and social media, data has become the new treasure that organizations must protect at all costs.

DBAs are a company's first line of defense in protecting this treasure. Their job is to devise and implement security measures so that sensitive data does not

At a Glance

Database Administrator

Minimum Educational Requirements
Bachelor's degree in database administration, computer science, computer information systems, information technology, or a related field

Personal Qualities
Analytical thinker; excellent problem-solving ability; above-average communication skills

Certification
Recommended

Working Conditions
Indoors

Salary Range
About $75,800 to $127,616

Number of Jobs
As of 2016, about 119,500

Future Job Outlook
Growth rate of 11 percent through 2026

fall into the hands of hackers and cybercriminals. DBAs manage the databases that store and organize sensitive data. They also work with nontechnical staff, such as senior managers, to find out what sort of information is most important to the organization. Finally, DBAs figure out what types of database features users need and develop ways to use these features easily and securely.

A big part of the job is planning for natural disasters and cyberattacks. DBAs must be prepared to recover data in the event of a problem, which can be anything from a system glitch to a wildfire or hurricane that cuts off power. Most recoveries occur as a result of application software error and/or human error. No matter what the cause, DBAs must act quickly to preserve the data.

In their day-to-day work, most DBAs focus on three vital security tasks: authentication, or arranging for new user accounts; authorization, or establishing what are called permission profiles, which limit the areas of the database that people can access; and auditing, or tracking what has occurred in the database and who was responsible for the action. Auditing is particularly vital. DBAs who are employed by highly regulated industries—such as health care, finance, energy, and public utilities—must comply with stringent auditing rules and regulations. In fact, the Health Insurance Portability and Accountability Act requires that health care providers keep track of anyone who touches any data in a health care record, down to the row and line. In addition to these responsibilities, DBAs may assume even more tasks in small companies. They may sometimes take care of the help desk as well as perform backup and recovery or system upgrades.

With all of these exacting responsibilities, some people consider DBA work to be stressful. Todd Boss, a DBA with more than twenty years of experience, thrives on the stress and pressure. "You're constantly asked to problem-solve new and different things," he explained in a 2017 interview on the website Quora. "There are not too many jobs out there that can say this. One week you may be trying to dig into some puzzling performance problem, the next week you're solving a security issue, the next week you're planning for some future upgrade." Ntirety, an information technology (IT) company that provides database services to organizations, agrees with Boss's assessment. "There's a lot of talk about how hard it is to be a database administrator today—and it certainly can be a tough job," admitted a writer for Ntirety in a 2016 blog post. "But the job also offers numerous benefits. Between the plethora of job opportunities, growing salaries, and job flexibility, it's now a truly great time to be a DBA."

How Do You Become a Database Administrator?

Education

Individuals in this field must hold a bachelor's degree in database administration, computer science, computer information systems, IT, or a related field. Employers may prefer candidates with a master of business administration (MBA) degree and a concentration in database management, computer information systems, or management information systems. According to the career website Indeed, DBAs may enhance their résumé with specialized training and certifications.

Even more vital than a formal degree, however, is to have experience working with databases. According to the Bureau of Labor Statistics (BLS), many DBAs first spend one to five years as database developers, database programmers, or data analysts. Experience in these roles enables DBAs to specialize in one or more database management systems, which can be very important on the job.

Certification

Database vendors offer a variety of professional certification programs that can help DBAs advance their careers while gaining valuable technical skills. Most database certificates are vendor specific, so DBAs will want to be certified by the company that makes their preferred software. If they have trouble deciding, a 2018 survey on the Job Boards website reported that the most important certificates for DBAs were IBM's certified database administrator, Microsoft's standard query language (SQL) certification, and Oracle's certified professional.

Internships and Volunteer Work

Database administration requires a lot of experience and involves sensitive customer data such as bank account information and Social Security and credit card numbers. Therefore, volunteer opportunities for beginners are limited. DBAs who help nonprofit organizations with database implementation or management on a volunteer basis tend to be retired from the workforce.

Still, some volunteer opportunities are available for college students who are working toward a computer science or management information systems degree. Ideally, these volunteers should have a strong interest in how technological systems can support the work of a particular organization. They also should have a passion for diving deep into the architecture of a database, helping build its features and functionality.

Many internships in database administration are paid, and they offer excellent experience for those working toward a computer science or related degree. Facebook, Microsoft, ExxonMobil, Salesforce, Amazon, Apple, Bloomberg, Yelp, VMware, and Google offer higher-than-average pay to interns, according to 2019 information from career websites Indeed.com and Glassdoor.

Still other internships immerse students in the fast-paced, highly respected world of tech. Microsoft, for example, offers a twelve-week summer internship program in which interns enjoy great perks, such as an on-site gym, health and fitness classes, and a thriving social scene. Interns are assigned a mentor and get the chance to work on real projects. To be eligible, students must be enrolled in college full-time for at least one semester. In a 2017 Glassdoor blog, one former database management intern at Microsoft commented favorably on his experience: "[I was given] meaningful intern projects working with a great diversity of teams. Microsoft has their hands on absolutely everything, so you get to talk to a lot of very smart and interesting people."

While these internships are highly coveted, less high-profile or profitable internships still offer valuable training in database management. In addition to learning important technical skills, interns get to meet experienced DBAs who can mentor them. After graduation, these mentors may even write letters of recommendation for their interns or steer them toward full-time positions.

Skills and Personality

DBAs must resolve complex issues, so attention to detail is an essential trait for these professionals to possess. So is a passion for solving problems. "The job requires not only technical know-how but also creativity and critical thinking skills," states Ntirety. "DBAs make decisions that can affect business operations of the entire company."

Despite this awesome responsibility and the excitement that can accompany it, DBAs must also perform routine tasks, such as backing up data or testing (and retesting) systems to check for security breaches. They look for threats both within the database (known as clear-box testing) and at the interface to the database (black-box testing). For this reason, they should be able to tolerate repetitive, sometimes tedious tasks. In addition, ongoing maintenance of a database requires being on call, so DBAs must be flexible, spontaneous, and available to work at a moment's notice.

Finally, it is critical to have clear, sharp communication skills since DBAs often work as part of a team. They must be able to talk about complex technical information to senior managers and project stakeholders, many of whom may not even understand how databases work. In large organizations, DBAs often manage several people and therefore need to be good at supervising others and handling conflict.

On the Job

Employers

DBAs work in both the public and private sectors. Hospitals, clinics, and other health care organizations employ DBAs to help store and monitor patient data. Online and brick-and-mortar retailers depend on DBAs to ensure that customers' financial records and shipping information are accurate and up to date. Online marketing companies also depend on DBAs to manage their data.

Working Conditions

DBAs usually work in offices or laboratories in comfortable surroundings. The business environment depends on the organization and its corporate culture, but most DBAs work in a casual atmosphere. Still, because many DBAs are thought of as part of an organization's management team, they may be required to dress like management, which means no jeans or sandals except on casual Fridays, when the dress code is relaxed.

Because they perform essential duties, such as managing and safeguarding computer databases, DBAs often work more than forty hours a week. They may need to put in time in the evenings, on weekends, or even on holidays to meet deadlines or solve time-critical problems.

Earnings

DBAs are well rewarded for their long hours and hard work. In a 2017 survey, *U.S. News & World Report* ranked the DBA position as the sixth-best technology job, and the position is usually very well compensated. The median annual salary for a DBA is $89,050, according to the BLS, and *U.S. News & World Report* says that DBAs in the upper quartile of the profession can expect to make $103,500 and up. The job offers above-average opportunities for advancement and salary increases.

Opportunities for Advancement

DBAs are often promoted to computer and information systems manager positions, which are also known as IT managers or IT project managers. IT managers supervise all computer-related activities and help senior management determine and achieve an organization's technical goals. According to Salary.com,

IT managers in the United States earned an average of $118,430 per year as of September 2018, in a range that typically falls between $105,951 and $130,392, depending on years of experience, certifications, and leadership skills.

After serving as IT managers, some ambitious employees climb to the highest rung of the career ladder and become chief information officers (CIOs). CIOs are among an organization's top decision makers and strategists. They make big decisions regarding the purchase of various types of software and hardware. They supervise other staff within the IT department, and they collaborate with other executives. To obtain this high-level position, an MBA is highly desirable. The median salary for a CIO is $154,614, according to the BLS.

What Is the Future Outlook for Database Administrators?

The BLS predicts that employment of DBAs will grow by 11 percent through 2026. That is a faster rate than the average for all occupations and just a tick below the 12 percent growth rate projected by the agency for all computer-related jobs.

Find Out More

The Data Administration Newsletter (TDAN)

PO Box 112571
Pittsburgh, PA 15241
website: www.tdan.com

TDAN is an online publication that contains articles and other resources for data management professionals and those considering a career in the industry. It also includes an archive of companies and products, books and book reviews, and event listings.

Data Management International (DAMA)
website: www.dama.org

DAMA is a not-for-profit global association of technical and business professionals. Its website contains information about academic and training programs in data management, an extensive data resource management bibliography, and information about its certified data management professional certification program.

International DB2 Users Group (IDUG)
330 N. Wabash Ave., Suite 2000
Chicago, IL 60611-4267
website: www.idug.org

An independent, not-for-profit organization, IDUG provides education and services to promote the use of DB2, IBM's database server product. The organization holds industry conferences and technical seminars.

SearchDataManagement
website: http://searchdatamanagement.com

SearchDataManagement is a website that provides news, learning guides, expert advice, and webcasts to data management professionals. The site offers independent and vendor-produced content about various database management products. It also has a large archive of articles and podcasts of interest to IT professionals and those seeking a career in data management.

Website Developer

The websites that people scan, the products they order, and the online news they consume are all made available by website developers. These talented, multifaceted professionals combine artistic flair with computer programming to create websites for large and small businesses, government agencies, schools, colleges, and other organizations. They lay out content so it is visually appealing, and they select color palettes and make other design decisions. Then, using their technical expertise, they make sure a website performs its best.

Some website developers take care of all facets of development and upkeep. Using a variety of programming languages and web technologies, they design a site with pleasing graphics, which often include animation. They also manage how well the site works and what features it offers, and they implement tools (such as the ability to comment on a product or put items in a shopping cart). They are responsible for the look of the site as well as its technical aspects, including its performance and capacity, which are measures of a site's speed and how much traffic it can handle.

Website developers focus on either the front end, or client side

At a Glance

Website Developer

Minimum Educational Requirements
High school diploma

Personal Qualities
Creative; problem-solving skills; detail oriented

Certification
Recommended

Working Conditions
Indoors

Salary Range
About $36,830 to $122,320

Number of Jobs
As of 2016, about 162,900

Future Job Outlook
Growth rate of 15 percent through 2026

(what consumers look at), or the back end, or server side (the hidden programming and structure that make the website functional). Developers who focus on the front end are often called web *designers*. Those who concentrate on the back end are sometimes called web *architects*. Human resources departments and technology professionals frequently use all three titles—*developer*, *designer,* and *architect*—to describe the same position. However, students thinking about a career in web development must clearly understand the differences between front-end and back-end work. They should also start thinking about whether their natural abilities are better suited for one or the other.

Front-end development skills differ significantly from those needed for back-end development. Because they are responsible for how a website looks, front-end website developers have an innate interest in art and design. They create the site's layout, arrange graphics, integrate applications, and work with other content. They strive to build visually appealing sites that are easy to understand and navigate. An example of a creative front-end task is adding a digital shopping cart to a website. This would involve creating drop-down menus of product options, prices, and payment choices, all of which are built using computer programming languages such as HTML.

Whereas front-end website developers specialize in a site's design, appearance, and consumer-focused features such as product reviews and testimonials, back-end website developers focus on website security, structure, and content management. They create or improve back-end processes and codes and improve the server, the server-side applications, and databases that, when combined with front-end codes, contribute to a functional, friendly experience for the user.

Back-end website developers also study industry trends to improve how fast a website works and what users want most. An example of a trend is the use of chatbots (conversation software) on websites. Back-end website developers prefer problem solving to designing, and they possess a natural talent for math. As Nicole Ferguson writes in a 2018 article on the website Career Foundry, "If you enjoy working with data, figuring out algorithms and coming up with ways to optimize complex systems, you might prefer to work as a back-end developer."

In a way, back-end website developers act as enablers for their front-end counterparts. That is because a front-end website developer might create a beautifully crafted site, but if the application is slow, crashes often, or constantly throws error messages at users (all back-end problems), no one will care how good the site looks. An application's back end is responsible for functions like calculations, business logic, database interactions, and performance. Back-end code is run on the computer system's server. This means that back-end website developers need to understand not only programming languages and databases but server architecture as well.

A good-looking website starts with front-end website developers who use graphic-design tools such as Dreamweaver, Photoshop, and Illustrator. They also use web programming languages such as JS, HTML, and CSS, as well as CSS frameworks like Backbone, Bootstrap, and Foundation. In web design terms, a *framework* refers to a structure of files and folders of standardized code (HTML, CSS, JS documents, etc.) that serves as a basis for building a website. For the back end, website developers write code in various programming languages, including server-side JS, Ruby, Python, SQL, and PHP.

How Do You Become a Website Developer?

Education

Front-end website developers looking for a position at a small company or nonprofit organization do not necessarily need a four-year college degree. They are often evaluated more on their portfolios—the websites they have previously created—than on their formal education. "Employers in the software and media industries don't put much weight on degrees because many technological concepts are outdated by the time you graduate," writes Nick Pettit, a web designer, blogger, and teacher at Treehouse, an online code school. Still, a two-year associate's degree in website development or a similar discipline can help one land a front-end development job. Back-end development, on the other hand, is more technical and typically requires a bachelor's or even a master's degree in computer science or programming.

All website developers need to be fluent in HTML. In addition, most employers expect website developers to master other computer languages and know multimedia publishing tools such as Canva, a graphic-design program for creating images for blog posts and presentations. Because Internet technology changes so fast, website developers need to make sure they are always learning the latest programs.

Certification

Various organizations offer website development or design certifications as well as certification in computer languages. According to the website Business News Daily, popular web certifications include those from Adobe, Google, and Microsoft in addition to the Zend certified PHP engineer credential. Business News Daily recommends W3Schools's web certifications in HTML, CSS, JS, jQuery, PHP, and other languages. Students study for free and pay ninety-five dollars per topic to take an associated exam.

Another choice is to take classes at WebProfessionals.org. This organization offers certifications at the apprentice, associate, and professional levels, and it provides training through its Web Professional Academy program. A different organization, Learning Tree International, offers specialist and expert certifications in web development as well as a specialist certification in web design.

Volunteer Work and Internships

Internships and volunteer work provide high school students with a good opportunity to see whether website development is the career for them. Many students have already created at least one website in their spare time and have enough experience to design or redesign the site of a local nonprofit organization on a volunteer basis.

Internships—both paid and unpaid—are also a great way to acquire new skills. Even though some students may have enough experience to be paid for their work, many others land unpaid internships, and that is just fine: interning with a cutting-edge agency can prove to be beneficial in the long run. That is because website development interns can meet influential industry contacts who may help them throughout their entire careers.

Skills and Personality

Website developers must be excited about the Internet and eager to delve into its infinite options and opportunities. They should also enjoy lifelong learning; in the twenty-first century, technology changes quickly, and innovations are around every corner. Just as website developers need to think creatively and troubleshoot often, they also need to pay close attention to detail. Writing code requires extreme accuracy—even one incorrect character amid hundreds of thousands can crash a website. For this reason, website developers need to be able to focus on their work for hours at a time, often in solitude.

Lastly, website developers need to effectively communicate with their clients, who may be customers or executives. Developers must be able to interpret what the client needs from a business or fund-raising perspective and convey that message using compelling words and arresting graphics. John Arvisu, a self-employed front-end and back-end website developer in Mission Viejo, California, knows how important it is to clearly communicate with clients. "You have to ask lots of questions about what they want to accomplish with their site," he explained in a telephone interview with the author. "I listen carefully and take very good notes when talking with them. Being a good listener is one of the soft skills that is really important for a web developer."

On the Job

Employers

According to Upwork, a popular career search website, website developers are in high demand. They work for information technology consulting companies, small start-ups, large and local nonprofit organizations, and very large organizations like hospitals, banks, and Fortune 500 companies such as Qualcomm, Microsoft, Google, Facebook, and Nike. In addition, website developers work in the creative services departments of universities and government agencies. Website developers who work as contractors typically earn more money than their permanently employed counterparts. However, there is a trade-off: contractors do not receive employee benefits such as paid vacation or sick days, employer-covered health insurance, and retirement plans.

Industry research shows that about 25 percent of US website developers own their own businesses or work as freelancers. "There's never been a better time to build your very own web design business as a web professional," commented Troy Dean, the cofounder of WP Elevation and Video User Manuals, in a 2018 *Go Daddy* blog post. "The internet has changed the way we communicate, socialize and do business, and if you can help clients get online through your design or development skills, you're in a great position."

Working Conditions

Website developers work indoors, often in informal settings. Projects can have tight deadlines because they are tied to product launches or other time-sensitive issues. This requires website developers to put in long hours, often clocking forty to sixty hours a week. In fact, some developers need to put in time at night, over weekends, and even during holidays so that an organization's site can be tested without interrupting normal operations.

Earnings

According to the Bureau of Labor Statistics (BLS), the median annual wage for website developers in 2017 was $74,110. The top 10 percent earned more than $122,320, and the bottom 10 percent earned $36,830. Salary.com reported slightly higher earnings for 2018. The career site says that the average website developer salary in the United States was $79,055, but the range typically falls between $69,406 and $89,914.

Opportunities for Advancement

Because website developers perform specialized work and typically do not have management responsibility, they have few chances for upward mobility in a corporate or government setting. When they attain their highest salary, website developers often become managers of creative services departments or advance to project management roles.

What Is the Future Outlook for Website Developers?

According to the BLS, employment of website developers is projected to grow 15 percent through 2026, much faster than the average for all occupations. Demand will be driven by the growing popularity of mobile devices and e-commerce. In this digital era, people are highly dependent on smart gadgets, and the e-commerce industry is booming. According to a 2016 *Tech Crunch* blog post, 79 percent of people spend money shopping online, and that statistic grows every day.

Find Out More

American Institute of Graphic Arts (AIGA)
233 Broadway, Suite 1740
New York, NY 10279
website: www.aiga.org

As the largest community of design advocates and practitioners, the AIGA advocates for a greater understanding of the value of design and designers in government, business, and media. This industry organization also hosts a calendar of events as well as programming and initiatives to serve a wide range of special interest groups.

Graphic Artists Guild
31 W. Thirty-Fourth St., 8th Floor
New York, NY 10001
website: https://graphicartistsguild.org

The Graphic Artists Guild's primary purpose is to help its members build successful careers by equipping them with the skills and support needed to compete more effectively in an ever-changing field. The organization serves graphic and interactive designers, illustrators, animators, web programmers, and developers.

International Web Association (IWA)
556 S. Fair Oaks Ave., Suite 101-200
Pasadena, CA 91105
website: http://iwanet.org

The IWA is one of the leading organizations for web professionals. It provides educational resources, a certification program, and professional networking opportunities for its members. Its website offers a list of job profiles and professional standards.

National Association of Programmers
PO Box 529
Prairieville, LA 70769
website: www.napusa.org

The National Association of Programmers is dedicated to programmers, developers, consultants, and other professionals and students in the computer industry. The group's goal is to provide information and resources to its members so they have a competitive edge in the computer industry.

WebDeveloper.com
website: www.webdeveloper.com

WebDeveloper.com is a free online discussion forum that covers all aspects of web development, including front-end and back-end development, design, site management, and business issues. The site is a gathering place for web development professionals to share knowledge and advice. It is also a resource for those new to the field of web development.

Mobile App Developer

Mobile devices—and the ever-increasing number of applications (apps) they run—are changing the way that people communicate, do business, and access news and entertainment. Companies, consumers, and programmers thrive on this method of communication, making the position of mobile app developer one of the most in-demand and fast-growing information technology (IT) careers, according to the tech site IT Career Finder.

Mobile app developers are a type of software developer. They specialize in building apps for mobile technologies such as tablets and smartphones. Mobile app developers who work on smartphones might specialize in Google's Android, Apple's iOS, or Microsoft's Universal Windows Platform. Depending on which platform they work with, their job title might be something like Android developer, iOS developer, or hybrid mobile developer.

At a Glance

Mobile App Developer

Minimum Educational Requirements
Bachelor's degree; master's degree for some upper-level positions

Personal Qualities
Ability to interpret and follow technical plans; problem-solving skills; determination and enthusiasm to learn the latest technology developments and trends

Certification
Recommended

Working Conditions
Indoors

Salary Range
About $73,877 to $112,500

Number of Jobs
As of 2017, about 162,900

Future Job Outlook
Growth rate of 24 percent through 2026

Each mobile platform has its own core languages. Apps that run on Android are usually programmed in Java, currently the most popular programming language in the world, according to the tech website the Tool. While Java requires a lot of coding, there is an alternative: Kotlin. The Tool says this coding language is easier for developers to read, and coding can be done more efficiently.

Apple's first mobile app development language—Objective-C—was useful for creating apps on several devices. A more recent programming language is Swift, which is easier for developers to use and more accurate for checking software errors. Microsoft's Universal Windows Platform uses various programming languages, including C++, C#, and Visual Basic. These languages change often to keep up with the pace of new technology. That is why aspiring mobile app developers need to stay aware of the latest offerings. One good source for industry trends is the software developer website CodeMentor Community.

The demand for mobile app developers across platforms has never been stronger. In 2018 mobile and tablet devices accounted for a higher percentage of Internet usage than did desktop computers, according to the digital marketing website Smart Insights. People tend to load up their smartphones with mobile gaming apps—62 percent of users reportedly install a game within a week of purchasing a phone, according to Smart Insights. Popular apps include YouTube, Kik, Telegram, Tumblr, ASKfm, Instagram, and Snapchat.

"Whether you're Snapchatting with friends or catching Pokémon, you probably spend time every day using the creations of mobile app developers," the website CNN Money reported in its 2017 *Best Jobs in America* report. "They aren't necessarily saving the world, but mobile app developers get to create something that can reach millions of people on a daily basis. That means growing demand for developers." That demand is reflected in the fact that, according to the *Wall Street Journal*, Apple and Google offer more than seven hundred thousand mobile apps each. ABI Research reports that total revenue in the mobile app industry is expected to significantly rise over the next few years. Mobile app developers with the right mix of skills can potentially find unlimited opportunity in this multibillion-dollar industry.

Although working as a mobile app developer may seem like all fun and games, these tech professionals have many serious responsibilities. These include developing application programming interfaces to make sure the apps perform well on mobile devices; keeping up to date with the terminology, concepts, and best practices for coding mobile apps; using and adapting existing web applications for apps; and working closely with their colleagues to constantly innovate app functionality and design. Companies—especially retailers—use mobile apps to alert their customers to sales, special promotions, and loyalty programs, for example. It is up to the developer to make these apps interesting and easy for customers to use.

How Do You Become a Mobile App Developer?

Education

Application developers usually have a bachelor's degree in computer science or software engineering. Degrees of this type require a student to concentrate in areas such as data structuring, system design, or programming. Because learning computer languages is important, many computer science programs make these language classes part of the major's core curriculum. A few advanced positions require candidates to have a master's degree in computer science or software engineering. Master's degree programs follow a more specific kind of application, such as Internet program development.

When choosing an education program for mobile app development, the IT Career Finder recommends that students take classes in iOS application development (for the iPhone and iPad), Android application development, object-oriented programming, Java programming, and game and simulation programming. The job search website Dice reports that there are numerous boot camps, mobile app developer training programs, and accredited degree programs that feature course work in mobile app programming, mobile media design, app deployment, and marketing. The education site Course Report also lists a wide range of boot camps and training programs.

Certification

"Although not all job descriptions expect mobile app development certifications, having a certification definitely adds spotlight in your résumé or qualifies you for promotion," reported the IT consulting firm Red Bytes in a June 2018 blog post. Red Bytes reports that the Android certified application developer, Salesforce's certified platform app builder, and native mobile application developer certifications are the most requested credentials for mobile app developers. Instruction and testing are available through a wide variety of online schools, and many tech companies—including Google, Microsoft, Apple, SAP, and Salesforce—offer courses on their own products.

Internships

Many large tech companies offer internship programs that come with competitive salaries, mentorships, and learning opportunities. For example, Facebook pays its interns well, and it gives them further opportunities to connect with others in the industry by inviting them to hackathons, off-site events, and weekly question-and-answer sessions with executives. Paid internships at smaller companies range from $15 an hour to $45,000 a year, according to the Glassdoor website. Even if internships are unpaid, they offer excellent on-the-job experience, valuable opportunities to network with industry professionals, and solid references for future permanent employment.

Skills and Personality

Mobile app developers should have a passion for solving problems and learning new technologies, according to tech writer Faye Bridge. "You should have the ability to balance thinking about both the big picture and the small details," she wrote in a 2016 Treehouse blog. "You must also be curious and inquisitive because when your code works (or it doesn't), you need to not be afraid to ask 'why' and keep digging till you find the answer."

Math skills are critical, but different applications require different types of math expertise. Basic layouts and designs require simple algebra skills. When working with complicated graphics, however, algebra, geometry, and trigonometry are important, as are abstract critical-thinking skills, according to Tom Park, a veteran mobile app developer in San Francisco. "Students who do not enjoy or who are not skilled in higher math should consider working in visual layout, which is a lot simpler than distributed systems [working on a network of computers]," Park said in a telephone interview with the author. "Fortunately, there is a whole spectrum of tasks in mobile app development," he added. "If students attempt the harder stuff, and it's not for them, they can move down the ladder and work on simpler applications."

In addition to math skills, developers must also have good people skills. They should be able to relate to both their clients and their team members. They must also possess empathy because developing software ultimately requires thinking about how people use technology and what they need. For this reason, the ability to understand users offers mobile app developers valuable and essential perspective.

On the Job

Employers

Many newly graduated mobile app developers dream of working for IT giants such as Google, Microsoft, Apple, Facebook, and Salesforce. But the technology divisions of various other Fortune 500 companies usually have many mobile app developer positions open as well. For example, the popular brick-and-mortar retailer Macy's has an online division (macys.com) that hires developers in its New York and San Francisco offices. The prepaid credit card company Card.com also hires mobile app developers, as do the online gaming and video company Twitch and numerous other companies and organizations across nearly every industry.

Not all mobile app developers take a full-time, permanent position with a company, however. Many take projects on a contract

Mobile app developers review the look and functionality of a program that will be accessible on smartphones. Mobile app development is one of the most in-demand and fast-growing IT careers.

or freelance basis. These types of projects can last anywhere from a few weeks to several years. Contract work usually pays more than full-time employment, but benefits such as vacation and retirement are not included.

Working Conditions

Mobile app developers work indoors, often in a casual environment. Most work full-time, and overtime is often required to meet deadlines. Freelance developers can choose their own hours, and many work part-time.

The BHW Group, a consulting firm that develops mobile apps, is an example of a fun and rewarding work environment. In both 2016 and 2017, BHW was voted one of the best places to work in Austin, Texas, because of its warm, friendly environment and focus on teamwork and communication. The popular company has a laid-back atmosphere that makes new workers feel comfortable. Companies with casual atmospheres and friendly work environments help tech workers stay passionate about the apps they are developing.

Earnings

According to Dice, an iOS developer with five years of experience can earn $83,500 to $112,500 in San Francisco; an Android developer with the same experience in the same city will earn slightly less, between $76,500 and $104,000. iPhone developers tend to make more than their Android counterparts because iPhone apps cost more money.

Opportunities for Advancement

To advance in this career, mobile app developers can become chief information officers (CIOs). CIOs are responsible for making their organization's biggest decisions, directing strategy, supervising other staff within the IT department, and collaborating with other executives. To obtain this high-level position, a mobile app developer typically needs to earn a master of business administration degree. Although pursuing another degree takes time and money, those who do so are well rewarded: the median salary for a CIO is $154,614, according to the Bureau of Labor Statistics (BLS).

What Is the Future Outlook for Mobile App Developers?

The BLS does not keep separate statistics for this particular job, but software developers—a category that includes mobile app developers—have a strong projected growth overall, and the BLS predicts that these developers will see a job growth rate of 24 percent through 2026. This category is growing because almost every single industry needs employees who know how to write code, according to Ken Mazaika, a chief technology officer. "Companies are willing to pay a lot of money for developers who can solve their core business problems," he said in a 2017 post on the website Quora.

ACT: The App Association
website: http://actonline.org

As a professional association, ACT represents more than five thousand companies and freelance professionals across the United States. It focuses specifically on the development of mobile apps and is one of the first professional organizations to focus on the mobile side of the IT industry.

Association of Software Professionals
website: https://asp-software.org

The Association of Software Professionals is one of the oldest and most established professional associations for software development. Its various newsletters and libraries of digitized information make it a valuable resource for students and young professionals who are just getting started.

Developers Alliance
1015 Seventh St. NW, 2nd Floor
Washington, DC 20001
website: www.developersalliance.org

The Developers Alliance supports the professional and academic needs of current and future software developers. Its focus is not specifically on mobile platforms but rather on software development overall. Still, hundreds of its members work in mobile app development, producing innovative, outside-the-box solutions to contemporary technological issues.

Girls Who Code
website: https://girlswhocode.com

Girls Who Code offers free after-school programs for girls in middle and high school. This nonprofit organization was founded in 2012 with a single mission: to close the gender gap in technology. It has now become a movement reaching almost ninety thousand girls of all backgrounds in all fifty states.

Business Intelligence Analyst

What Does a Business Intelligence Analyst Do?

Every day, companies accumulate enormous amounts of data from their customers. This data pertains to purchasing—what people buy, when they buy it, and how much money they spend. The information flows in from various sources, including loyalty card programs, social media, mobile apps, credit cards, and even satellite imagery such as Google Earth and Google Maps. Collecting all of this data is one task—using it to learn more about customers' tendencies is another.

Business intelligence analysts (BIAs) help companies interpret the data they collect, with the goals of increasing efficiency and maximizing profits. BIAs spend much of their time examining data to identify company weaknesses and find solutions to problems. For that reason, BIAs straddle the worlds of

At a Glance

Business Intelligence Analyst

Minimum Educational Requirements
Bachelor's degree in information technology, information systems, or computer science

Personal Qualities
Analytical; business focused; excellent communication and presentation skills

Certification
Recommended

Working Conditions
Indoors

Salary Range
About $56,143 to $79,352

Number of Jobs
As of 2017, about 162,380

Future Job Outlook
Growth rate of 21 percent through 2024

business and information technology (IT). By having a firm foothold in each, they are able to mine and analyze data to recommend growth strategies for a company.

An example of how BIAs can help improve a company's performance comes from RTS Labs, a management consulting firm in Virginia. One of the firm's clients, an online retailer, needed to more effectively use its marketing budget. The client had learned how customers purchased its products, but it needed to better organize and analyze the information to understand whether its marketing program was working. The BIA at RTS Labs categorized the client's customers on the basis of various factors, including age, how often they shopped, and what products they bought most often. Using this data, the BIA was able to generate a list of customers to target with e-mail offers. "The result was a decreased number of emails marked as spam, a three-fold surge in response to marketing initiatives, a 30 percent reduction in customer churn rates, and a 60 percent reduction in marketing costs," reports RTS Labs on its website.

Whether BIAs work as consultants or employees, their job is to comb through large amounts of data to learn more about a company's customers; for example, how often do they buy a certain product? Does a certain age group (teens, for instance) buy the product more than another group? BIAs then produce reports in which they identify trends to help a company make better business decisions. These reports provide a clear view of business operations and pinpoint potential improvements for everything from how a company advertises its services to how fast it ships its products to the way it follows up with customers on social media.

For BIAs, a major part of their job is to recommend what new systems or business practices will best fit a company. They also suggest how to improve employment and staffing issues. They identify inefficient business methods and recommend alternatives and/or suggest solutions to specific business problems, such as how to increase market share or beat out the competition. After BIAs make such recommendations, they often lead training sessions for clients or colleagues on how best to make the change and monitor its impact. Because of their ability to critically impact a company's revenues, BIAs work closely with a company's department heads, high-level executives, and any other senior management.

Many BIAs carefully plan their career paths while still in college. Others, however, stumble into their dream jobs quite accidentally. Such was the case for Sonya Fournier, a BIA with the management consultant firm PMSquare in Nova Scotia, Canada. Fournier initially obtained a bachelor's degree in history, and she then took a position in retail. While working in retail, she became intrigued with computer systems and discovered she was good with data. She then heard about a degree program at a technical school and decided to enroll. After graduating, Fournier took a computer analyst position in Boston and has continued up the BIA ladder ever since. "When I was in high school, I didn't even know that a job like business intelligence analyst existed," she said in a 2017 blog post for the Datapine company. "That's why I tell young people to keep their options open about a career in IT. They may be perfect for a job that doesn't even exist right now."

How Do You Become a Business Intelligence Analyst?

Education

BIAs usually have a bachelor's degree in information systems, computer science, data science, business administration, engineering, or economics. Although a master of business administration degree is preferred, it is not required if candidates have sufficient work experience and enough certifications. Perhaps most importantly, aspiring BIAs need to understand how data is collected and used. For that reason, they should take classes in data architecture, database design, data mining, and data visualization, and they should learn to use software tools such as Tableau and Qlik. They should also be familiar with data security and privacy issues.

Certification

One of the best professional certifications for BIAs is Microsoft's certified solutions expert in business intelligence, according to the online career college Discover Data Science (DDS). DDS recommends that aspiring BIAs also pursue the Data Warehousing Institute's certified business intelligence professional designation at either the practitioner or mastery level. However, candidates will need at least two years of relevant work experience to register for this exam. Another valuable certification is the certified business analysis professional (CBAP), obtained through the International Institute of Business Analysis. BIAs with at least three years of experience in their profession are eligible to take the comprehensive exam.

Internships

Trying to gain BIA experience by volunteering is not possible for college students because most organizations need a seasoned analyst rather than a beginner. Internships, on the other hand, abound. Because business intelligence is such a vital, growing field, both paid and unpaid internships are available at a wide variety of companies, universities, nonprofit organizations, and government agencies, according to the career website Indeed. These organizations range from entertainment giants such as Sirius XM Satellite Radio, movie studios like Universal and Lionsgate, sportswear leader Nike, large insurance companies, digital marketing agencies, management consulting firms, and even the Central Intelligence Agency (CIA). Paid internships range from about seventeen dollars an hour for part-time work to about thirty-five dollars an hour for summer jobs. Many large companies also offer their interns paid medical insurance, gym memberships, and other perks. However, in most cases, interns must pay for their own housing and relocation.

Even unpaid internships offer aspiring BIAs vital experience and exposure to the dynamic field of business intelligence. These benefits include one-on-one mentorships from seasoned BIAs, opportunities to expand one's technical and business knowledge, and connections with other interns, recent graduates, employees,

Business intelligence analysts go over a client's sales data. Their assessment of that data will be used to help the client with future business decisions.

and senior management. "An internship is a strong avenue for gaining the necessary skills, experience, and perspective to successfully move forward," says Brian Green, a San Diego–based business intelligence analyst.

Skills and Personality

Unlike other IT positions, which mainly require people to have excellent software skills and technological expertise, BIAs need to possess both technical skills and business knowledge. Perhaps the most important quality BIAs need is to be passionate about data in its many forms and facets. They must also excel in data mining, which is the process of sorting through large data sets or information to identify patterns, which enables enterprises to predict future trends about a business and its customers.

Once BIAs collect and interpret the business data, they must communicate the information to their team members and to senior management in a way that people who lack technical skills can understand. This is why BIAs need to have excellent communication and presentation skills, according to technology writer Laura Brandenburg. "This means they can facilitate working meetings, ask good questions, listen to the answers (really listen), and absorb what's being said," she explained in a 2017 blog post on the education site Bridging the Gap. In addition, they must be problem solvers and critical thinkers who can see the big picture while carefully managing a myriad of technical details.

On the Job

Employers

According to the Bureau of Labor Statistics (BLS), 17 percent of BIAs are self-employed and work as consultants. The remaining 83 percent work for medium and large businesses that collect and manage varying degrees of big data. The industries that are currently hiring the most BIAs include finance, insurance, tech, and health care. Many BIAs work in large cities such as Washington, DC; New York City; Chicago; and Atlanta, where such industries are headquartered.

BIAs who are self-employed can either find clients on their own, through their business networking contacts, or by working through a recruiting agency such as Robert Half, a global job-placement firm with a strong technology focus. "There's a growing demand for candidates who are highly skilled in analytics, who can interpret data, and generate deeper insight that leads to better decision making," reports a February 2018 blog post on the Robert Half website.

Working Conditions

BIAs work indoors, often in a corporate setting. Much of this time is spent working independently at one's desk because there is so much data to decipher. As IT consultant Say Keng Lee said in a 2018 Quora blog post, BIAs spend "most of their time in the backroom mining and analyzing data, past and present." Most BIAs work full-time, and overtime is often required so that deadlines can be met. Self-employed BIAs can choose their own hours, and many work part-time.

Earnings

The salary range for BIAs is about $56,143 to $79,352, with an average salary of $66,000, according to the website PayScale.

Opportunities for Advancement

Because of their combined knowledge of business and technology, BIAs are highly valued by their organizations. In addition, their regular contact with management gets them noticed by their company's most senior people, who frequently decide who gets promoted. For these reasons, BIAs often move into higher-level jobs within ten years, including roles such as analytics manager, business intelligence manager, business intelligence architect, and analytics manager, according to DDS.

What Is the Future Outlook for Business Intelligence Analysts?

The job market for BIAs is expected to grow by 21 percent through 2024, according to the BLS. BIAs are required in many different fields, including health care, education, finance, and law enforcement. Organizations in these fields and others are looking for ways to compete and/or optimize customer service, and BIAs can provide key data-based insights to create these advantages. Thus, they are highly sought-after individuals. "Provided you have the right skills, experience, and interest in solving problems, you will be able to set yourself apart in this competitive, yet thriving job market," says DDS.

Find Out More

Business Analyst Times
website: www.batimes.com

This free website offers in-depth articles, blogs, white papers, job listings, webinars, and other resources about business/systems analysis, industry events, and cutting-edge business analysis insights. It also provides information on obtaining a CBAP certification.

Digital Analytics Association (DAA)

401 Edgewater Pl., Suite 600
Wakefield, MA 01880
website: www.digitalanalyticsassociation.org

The DAA's goal is to advance the use of data to understand and improve the digital world through professional development and community. Its website contains information about education, certification, jobs, and more.

International Institute of Business Analysis (IIBA)

115 George St., Suite 509
Oakville, ON L6J 0A2 Canada
website: www.iiba.org

The IIBA is a nonprofit professional association dedicated to the field of business analysis. Through a global network, the institute connects over twenty-nine thousand individual members, more than three hundred corporate members, and 120 chapters. As the voice of the business analysis community, the IIBA supports recognition of the profession and works to maintain the global standard for the practices and certification.

Modern Analyst Media

26500 W. Agoura Rd., Suite 102-711
Calabasas, CA 91302
website: www.modernanalyst.com

Modern Analyst Media offers various forums, directories, and other resources for business analysts to grow their businesses.

Strategic and Competitive Intelligence Professionals (SCIP)

7550 W. Interstate 10, Suite 400
San Antonio, Texas 78229
website: www.scip.org

SCIP is a global community of business experts from industry, academia, and the government who build and share strategic intelligence and research decision-support tools, processes, and analytics capabilities.

Cloud Solutions Architect

What Does a Cloud Solutions Architect Do?

Every day, people use cloud-based computer operations without necessarily realizing it. Teens use cloud-based technology when they communicate with friends over Snapchat, Instagram, Gmail, or WhatsApp. They also use cloud-based services when they stream movies on Netflix and upload videos to YouTube. These services and more are made possible by cloud computing, which is the practice of storing regularly used computer data on multiple servers that can be accessed through the Internet.

The cloud saves companies money. Instead of purchasing expensive hardware such as network servers and installing them at their offices, companies can simply get the data storage they need from a cloud vendor's remote servers by way of the Internet. By using the cloud, companies also save money on expensive software such as inventory control programs,

At a Glance

Cloud Solutions Architect

Minimum Educational Requirements
Bachelor's degree, preferably in computer science or a related discipline

Personal Qualities
Strong analytical abilities; effective project-management skills

Certification
Recommended

Working Conditions
Indoors

Salary Range
About $85,000 to $162,000

Number of Jobs
As of 2016, about 162,700

Future Job Outlook
Growth rate of 13 percent through 2026

which keep track of products in stock. When expensive software programs become outdated, companies do not need to pay for new versions. Instead, their cloud vendor replaces and updates the software when necessary. In exchange for these services, companies pay user fees.

Cloud solutions architects (CSAs) are responsible for keeping cloud applications up and running. They set up cloud computing functions based on their company's needs, which may include storing documents and e-mails, entering sales orders, keeping track of inventory, managing customer records, taking care of payroll, and making payments. They also create and develop Internet-based computing tools, such as video conferencing platforms. They are in charge of maintaining these systems and troubleshooting problems that arise. In a large organization, a CSA may have a team of workers who do the actual day-to-day monitoring. In a smaller company, the CSA may be the only person who performs these tasks.

Regardless of company size, CSAs do much more than just design systems or troubleshoot a company's online operations. "A cloud architect focuses more on the meta, or big-picture, view of the data center and less on an individual server's configuration," explained technology reporter Paul Korzeniowski in a 2017 blog on the information technology (IT) website TechTarget. "Rather than get caught up in the daily grind of data center and cloud operations, cloud architects must think ahead. They need to be blue-sky, big-picture thinkers."

As "big-picture thinkers," CSAs must focus on key business trends as well as the latest technology offerings. On the business side, they need to figure out which computer programs will help their company increase sales. One example is a customer relationship management (CRM) program, which helps companies track and analyze their interactions with existing and potential customers. For several years CRM programs were located on a company's own computer system. Now, many of them reside in the cloud. "There's no doubt the future of CRM lies in the cloud," wrote tech reporter Lindsay Clark in a 2016 *Computer Weekly* blog post.

Once CSAs decide that their company's CRM software should be located in the cloud, they recommend to senior management which cloud vendor to use—say, for example, either Amazon Web Services (AWS), Microsoft's Azure, or Google Cloud. Then they are responsible for making sure the service is set up right and performs well. CSAs may also negotiate contracts and work alongside legal and purchasing departments.

How Do You Become a Cloud Solutions Architect?

Education

Most CSAs need to obtain a bachelor of science degree in a technical field such as computer science, software engineering, or math. A master of science degree is often preferred, but it is not required. A master of business administration (MBA) degree could be helpful for positions that require CSAs to recommend business strategies to senior management or executive-level clients. "Digital transformation is forcing IT to focus more closely on business partners' needs," said Meg Ramsey, the vice president of cloud services at Sungard Availability Services, in a February 2018 *CIO* magazine article. "Pursuing an MBA helps IT professionals broaden their experience and provides them with a holistic view of how the company operates."

In addition to a college degree, it is useful to have a strong background in scripting and to know several programming languages. A few of the languages that employers typically want job candidates to know are SQL, XML, Python, Java, C++, Bash, Node, PHP, Ruby on Rails, and Docker.

Certification

For CSAs, the certificate of cloud security knowledge is "the mother of all cloud computing security certifications," according to *CIO* magazine. Students can test for this certificate online, after paying a $395 fee. The most popular cloud certification is AWS's certified solutions architect, according to IT website Hacker Noon. "AWS is quickly becoming the gold standard of the cloud and leading the pack in almost every aspect," wrote software engineer Moneer Rifai in a 2017 blog post on the website. "Amazon's cloud is 10 times bigger than its next 14 competitors, combined!" Other than AWS, Microsoft offers various cloud certifications. In fact, Microsoft Virtual Academy offers free courses and training materials on many topics related to cloud technology.

In addition, many online schools, including Cloud Academy, Cloud Guru, and Udemy, offer cloud certification courses for a fee. In addition, AWS offers free digital training, allowing users to learn 150 AWS cloud skills at their own pace. Formal AWS courses are also available for a fee. Meanwhile, IBM offers two different certification programs: one on cloud computing architecture and the other on cloud computing infrastructure. Microsoft and Google also offer various online cloud certifications for a fee.

Volunteer Work and Internships

College students pursuing a bachelor's or master's degree in computer science or a related field can do a paid internship at a wide variety of organizations. Fortune 500 companies such as Google, Facebook, and Microsoft open their internship applications in September and fill most positions by November. At large companies, cloud computing interns are often asked to assist with a team project or take on a smaller portion of a large project. In either case, the intern typically has access to a project leader who can answer questions and provide guidance.

Tech companies do not usually hire volunteers to perform cloud computing work because of the high level of experience required. Still, a high-visibility volunteer opportunity exists on the website of the Institute of Electrical and Electronics Engineers (IEEE), which hosts the IEEE Cloud Computing Community. This is a key platform for researchers, academicians, and industry practitioners who share and exchange ideas regarding cloud computing technologies and services. The organization regularly seeks volunteer bloggers. By blogging on this site, aspiring CSAs can gain visibility and credibility, which could lead to a paid position.

Skills and Personality

CSAs must be self-driven, collaborative thinkers who enjoy solving problems. They should be passionate about helping companies grow their business by using the latest online tools. They should also thrive on working with cutting-edge technologies to test and expand their skills.

CSAs must also communicate well and enjoy working on a team. After all, this role is about understanding the needs of computer users, providing advice, managing risks, and delivering useful technological results and products. The position may also require one to work closely with business decision makers, business analysts, project teams, vendor representatives, and many other roles. Therefore, CSAs need to be able to listen, empathize, explain, advise, influence, and negotiate, all while navigating complex technologies. They also need to possess impressive people skills, be tactful and diplomatic, and remain grounded in their technical expertise. "The best solution architects will give the right advice for the business result required," explained Mindi Clews in a 2015 blog post on the website of Equinox IT, a tech consulting company. "This may mean standing firm on a decision and not being persuaded by vendor hype, product claims, or silver bullets. This may also mean telling organizations the hard facts that they may not want to hear."

On the Job

Employers

Most CSA positions are not entry level in nature. Still, a recent computer science graduate can obtain a junior-level IT position and become a CSA in a few years. A good way to accomplish this is to work for an IT consulting company on a contract basis (rather than having a full-time, in-house position). A contract project may last just a few weeks or span several years. Contract work usually pays more than full-time employment, but benefits such as vacation and retirement plans are not typically included. Some consulting companies hire CSAs on a full-time basis and move them from project to project.

Other CSAs work for large technology companies, including Salesforce, Infosys, ServiceNow, Dell, or SoftLayer. Still others work for global investment banks; large insurance and health care companies such as Aetna Digital; a wide variety of Fortune 500 companies, including Tesla, Verizon, and Liberty Mutual Global Risk Solutions; government agencies; and universities.

Working Conditions

CSAs work indoors and on-site if the employer is a Fortune 500 company, at the client's site if the employer is an IT consulting firm, or remotely from a home office. Overtime is often required so that project deadlines can be met. In addition, CSAs may spend up to 50 percent of their time traveling to various client locations and the remaining 50 percent at their headquarters.

Earnings

The Bureau of Labor Statistics (BLS) does not list specific salaries for CSAs because this specialty is relatively new. In 2017 the BLS listed $104,650 as the median pay for computer network architects with bachelor's degrees. According to the career website PayScale, enterprise IT architects with cloud computing expertise earned a median salary of $137,957 in 2017, and AT&T paid a median salary of $248,323 to experienced cloud computing professionals. Both the BLS and Payscale consider computer network architects and enterprise IT architects to be similar to CSAs.

Opportunities for Advancement

Since CSAs are already one of the highest-paid IT positions, the best opportunity for advancement is to become an executive-level manager, such as a chief technology officer, at a Fortune 500 company or large IT consulting firm. For a position like this, it would be important to have an MBA.

What Is the Future Outlook for Cloud Solutions Architects?

Cloud solutions architecture is considered a hot career field, and skilled, experienced CSAs are in demand all over the world. In fact, a 2017 study by *Forbes* magazine predicts that cloud computing is projected to account for $162 billion in annual business growth by 2020. The BLS predicts that employment of computer and information technology occupations will grow by 13 percent through 2026, faster than the average for all occupations. These occupations are projected to add about 557,100 new jobs. The demand for these workers will stem from a greater emphasis on cloud computing, the collection and storage of big data, and information security.

Find Out More

Cloud Computing Association (CCA)

79 Main St., 3rd Floor
Port Washington, NY 11050
website: www.cloudcomputingassn.org

The CCA is an independent membership organization dedicated to building a community of end users and service providers of cloud-based solutions and products. The organization's goal is to promote the adoption and use of cloud-based technologies across all industry sectors.

Cloud Security Alliance (CSA)

website: https://cloudsecurityalliance.org

This organization advocates for best practices to provide security assurance in cloud computing. Its objectives include promoting understanding, researching best practices, and launching awareness campaigns to create a consensus on ways to ensure cloud security. In addition, the CSA offers training and certifications, global events, regional chapter memberships, and blogs written by industry professionals.

IEEE Cloud Computing Community
website: www.ieee.org

This is the first broad-based collaborative project for the cloud to be introduced by the Institute of Electrical and Electronics Engineers (IEEE), a global professional association. This community provides coverage across multiple interdependent tracks. These include an IEEE web portal, a conference, continuing education courses, publications, standards, and a platform for testing cloud computing applications.

MSPAlliance
100 Europa Dr., Suite 403
Chapel Hill, NC 27517
website: https://mspalliance.com

The International Association of Cloud and Managed Service Providers (MSPAlliance) is the largest and oldest vendor-neutral organization for cloud and managed service providers. It has more than thirty thousand cloud computing and managed service provider corporate members around the globe. The organization offers conferences, expos, regional workshops, networking dinners, and training events.

Open Group
800 District Ave., Suite 150
Burlington, MA 01803
website: www.opengroup.org

The Open Group is a global consortium that enables the achievement of business objectives through technology standards. The diverse membership of more than 625 organizations includes customers, systems and solutions suppliers, tool vendors, integrators, academics, and consultants across multiple industries. Membership in this organization provides access to a wide variety of forums and work groups where members can network, gain relevant knowledge, grow professionally, and collaborate on the development of standards, best practices, and certifications.

Cybersecurity Analyst

What Does a Cybersecurity Analyst Do?

In a world where security guards protect company property and bodyguards protect people, it is the job of a cybersecurity analyst to protect an organization's data from theft, illegal duplication, and unauthorized access. Cybersecurity analysts protect data that exists on multiple platforms, including computer networks, servers, mobile devices, and payment software, to name a few. They also figure out where systems are vulnerable and develop ways to prevent them from being breached by cybercriminals, people who use the Internet to steal sensitive or private information from computer systems. Without the constant monitoring and analysis that cybersecurity analysts provide, businesses, public organizations, government agencies, and individuals are vulnerable to being hacked.

Cyberattacks take many forms, and it does not always take a seasoned cy-

At a Glance

Cybersecurity Analyst

Minimum Educational Requirements
Bachelor's degree in information technology, network security, computer information systems, computer science, or a related field

Personal Qualities
Good interpersonal skills; strong attention to detail; sound decision-making ability

Certification
Recommended

Working Conditions
Indoors

Salary Range
About $60,000 to $181,500

Number of Jobs
As of 2017, 105,250

Future Job Outlook
Growth rate of 28 percent through 2026

bercriminal to pull off a serious hack. In 2015, for example, fifteen-year-old Kane Gamble gained access to top-secret military operations in Afghanistan and Iran by pretending to be the head of the US Central Intelligence Agency (CIA). From the bedroom of his Leicestershire, England, home, Gamble used social engineering—a technique whereby scammers conceal their true identities and motives and present themselves as trusted individuals—to influence, manipulate, or trick users into giving up confidential information.

According to a January 2018 article in the London newspaper the *Daily Telegraph*, Gamble impersonated well-known US government officials to get passwords and gain highly private information. He obtained these passwords by calling the technology companies Verizon and AOL pretending to be then-CIA chief John Brennan and claiming he needed his password reset. Armed with Brennan's password, Gamble stole several sensitive documents from the CIA chief's e-mail inbox, accessed an intelligence database, and wreaked other havoc.

Cybersecurity analysts help protect against such actions. They maintain security for their organizations by conducting analytics and research and by learning to recognize suspicious online traffic. To do this, they work with penetration testing tools, which are attempts to evaluate the security of information technology (IT) infrastructure by safely trying to exploit vulnerabilities. These vulnerabilities may exist in operating systems, or services or applications may be flawed or improperly configured. Likewise, end users—the people for whom a software program or hardware device is designed—may engage in risky behavior, such as using the same password for several online accounts or clicking on a link in an e-mail without really knowing who sent it. Security testing—sometimes called ethical hacking—reveals such flaws and finds dangerous weaknesses hiding within software applications. After finding such vulnerabilities, cybersecurity analysts make recommendations to their company's systems administrator regarding what should change to keep corporate data safe.

Cybersecurity is more than just understanding basic security exploits. Cybersecurity analysts also need to know how to advise and communicate with executives about standards related to protecting data. This may sound exciting, but most of the time cybersecurity work is pretty routine. One typical task of a cybersecurity analyst is to ensure that computers are patched. A patch is a set of changes to a program or its supporting data that is designed to update, fix, or improve it. Cybersecurity analysts also audit logs and consult on a computer system's new products or features. They analyze phishing e-mails (which are sent by hackers and are intended to steal user data), manage firewalls (hardware or software systems that prevent unauthorized users from accessing private networks connected to the Internet), and manage intrusion detection systems, which are security software systems that automatically alert administrators when someone is trying to hack a computer system.

Even if cybersecurity analysts do a great job of protecting data, they still need the cooperation of the organization they are helping. "The biggest challenge cybersecurity professionals face today is companies (customers) who don't want to change their IT behaviors," commented IT security professional Chris Stoneff, the vice president of security solutions at Bomgar, an IT consulting company, in a 2018 blog post on Bomgar's website.

How Do You Become a Cybersecurity Analyst?

Education
Cybersecurity analysts need to have at least a bachelor's degree in computer science, programming, or a similar field. Some employers prefer candidates to have an advanced degree, such as a master of science in information assurance and cybersecurity. Those applying for a cybersecurity position with a military or government agency must often undergo a background check, obtain security clearances, and earn industry certifications. Prospective employers may offer tuition assistance to help employees obtain certain professional credentials.

Certification

To do their job, cybersecurity analysts must have expert knowledge of databases, networks, hardware, firewalls, and encryption. For this reason, certifications involving ethical hacking and the management and auditing of information security systems are extremely helpful. CompTIA's Security+ certificate, for example, only requires two years of IT experience and focuses on general cybersecurity issues.

After working in cybersecurity for at least five years, one of the best certifications for analysts to obtain is the Certified Information Systems Security Professional. This "is an advanced-level certification for IT pros serious about careers in information security," reported tech writers Ed Tittel and Kim Lindros in a 2018 Business News Daily article. In addition to the consortium, analysts can earn certificates from various online educational institutions, including the International Council of E-Commerce Consultants, also known as EC-Council; the New Horizons Computer Learning Centers; Florida Institute of Technology; Capella University; and others.

Volunteer Work and Internships

Cybersecurity administration is an advanced profession, and becoming an expert is a long-term, time-intensive venture. For this reason, volunteer opportunities at nonprofit organizations are often open only to retired professionals who have the required experience.

However, because cybersecurity is such a dynamic, in-demand profession, internships are abundantly available for college students pursuing computer science, information technology, and related degrees. Aerospace and defense companies are particularly interested in hiring cybersecurity interns, as is the Department of Homeland Security (DHS). In fact, this government agency's Cyber Student Volunteer Initiative extends summer opportunities to current undergraduate and graduate students nationwide. During these ten-week programs, student interns gain vital hands-on experience through challenging work projects, real-life scenarios, and mentoring from DHS cybersecurity professionals. Student assignments focus on areas such as identifying and analyzing malicious code, doing forensics analysis, handling incidents, and detecting and preventing intrusions. Cybersecurity internships are also available at Google, Apple, PricewaterhouseCoopers, Amgen, Amazon, VMware, Deloitte, Sony Pictures, Visa, PayPal, Microsoft, and many other large companies.

Skills and Personality

Cybersecurity analysts must be proficient in IT fundamentals (web applications and systems administration); able to code in C, C++, Java, PHP, Perl, Ruby, and Python; and well versed in computer architecture, administration, and operating systems. In addition to meeting educational qualifications, good interpersonal skills and general business expertise are important attributes to have. It is also critical to pay meticulous attention to detail because cybersecurity analysts routinely review log files that contain thousands of entries and configuration information from hundreds of devices.

Cybersecurity analysts must remain focused on the details. "An incorrect command sent to a device, or a single misspelling in a line of code could be disastrous," Robert Gaines, senior manager at Accume Partners, an IT consulting firm, commented in a 2017 Rasmussen College blog post. Employers also want cybersecurity analysts to have experience with multiple computer systems and programs, an aptitude for solving problems independently, and strong verbal and written communication skills.

On the Job

Employers

Cybersecurity analysts work in almost every industry that collects and stores large amounts of data. This includes government agencies, especially the DHS and the US military; government contractors; aerospace and defense firms; large finance and insurance companies; health care organizations (hospitals, medical device companies, and biotechnology companies); and technology giants such as Microsoft, Google, and Apple.

Working Conditions

Cybersecurity analysts work indoors and spend long hours at a computer conducting system analysis, monitoring real-time threats, and pursuing the organization's overall security strategy. The professional atmosphere depends on the organization's culture, but most cybersecurity analysts work in a casual office environment. Most work full-time and are often on-site after hours or on weekends so they can perform cybersecurity work without disrupting the work of other employees. "If you have a top level position, then the hours will be pretty intense," admitted Shane Elliott, a cybersecurity analyst at Razorfish, in a 2017 Quora blog post. "You'll be on-call for any issue that comes up, and you can't really ever completely be out of touch for vacations or holidays." Cybersecurity analysts with entry-level positions will likely work standard hours from about 9:00 a.m. to 6:00 p.m.

Earnings

Cybersecurity analysts fall into a category of professionals called information security analysts, which, as of May 2017, were earning an average annual salary of $99,690, according to the Bureau of Labor Statistics (BLS). The top 10 percent had earnings of more than $181,500. Salary potential and employment opportunities vary according to geographic location, market conditions, and an applicant's level of education and work experience.

Opportunities for Advancement

After a person has served as a cybersecurity analyst for two to three years, the next level of responsibility is chief information security officer (CISO). This middle-management position oversees the general operations of an organization's IT security division. CISOs are directly responsible for planning, coordinating, and directing all of the company's computer, network, and data security needs. They work directly with upper-level management to determine an organization's unique cybersecurity needs and are usually responsible for managing a staff of security professionals. According to a 2017 *Computerworld* blog, CISOs earn between $200,000 and $500,000 a year in total compensation.

What Is the Future Outlook for Cybersecurity Analysts?

According to the BLS, cybersecurity analyst jobs are projected to increase by 28 percent through 2026, much faster than the national average for all occupations. The demand for cybersecurity analysts is expected to be very high because more and more organizations need innovative solutions to prevent hackers from stealing critical information or causing problems for their computer networks.

Find Out More

Center for Internet Security (CIS)
website: www.cisecurity.org

The CIS delivers solutions and information for many security-related needs. It caters more to corporate entities (in both the public and private sectors) than to individuals. The organization provides resources for training and workforce development, compiles reports and case studies on industry topics, and offers various products and services.

CompTIA Association of Information Technology Professionals (AITP)
3500 Lacey Rd., Suite 100
Downers Grove, IL 60515
website: www.aitp.org

This global organization features webinars, conferences, local chapters, and awards for cybersecurity professionals and students. The AITP also offers a career center with a jobs board and plenty of networking options.

Forum of Incident Response and Security Teams (FIRST)

PO Box 1187
Morrisville, NC 27560-1187
website: www.first.org

As its name implies, FIRST is a forum that allows information security incident response teams to share their experiences, tips, and information. Beyond the forum itself, the organization holds technical workshops, meetings, and conferences. It also provides mailing lists and web repositories where teams can share information and other resources.

Information Systems Audit and Control Association (ISACA)

1700 E. Golf Rd., Suite 400
Schaumburg, IL 60173
website: www.isaca.org

ISACA is a global professional organization for information governance, control, security, and audit professionals. The standards set by ISACA are followed worldwide. The organization offers several professional certifications, industry publications, and conferences.

International Information Systems Security Certification Consortium

311 Park Place Blvd., Suite 400
Clearwater, FL 33759
website: www.isc2.org

The consortium is an international nonprofit membership association that provides education, exams, certifications, and seminars for information security leaders. Because of its more than 138,000 certified members, the consortium offers beginning cybersecurity analysts the opportunity to meet seasoned cybersecurity analyst professionals and even work together on certain projects.

Information Technology Consultant

Information technology (IT) jobs involve computer programming, data, and analysis. Many IT consultants work at consulting firms and act as external advisers to businesses on a range of IT issues, including product delivery, customer communication, and sales improvement.

Most projects begin by learning what hardware and software are already used and finding ways to make systems work better. For example, if an organization needs to switch to a new e-mail platform to cut costs, the IT consultant has to figure out which platform is most economical, determine how long it will take to change to the new platform, and then train employees on it. In doing this work, the IT consultant has

At a Glance

Information Technology Consultant

Minimum Educational Requirements
Associate's degree in computer science, information technology, or a related field

Personal Qualities
Superior technical expertise and a problem-solving aptitude; excellent communication and presentation skills

Certification
Recommended

Working Conditions
Indoors

Salary Range
About $83,860 to $175,890

Number of Jobs
As of 2017, about 365,690

Future Job Outlook
Growth rate of 12 percent through 2026

to think like a technician, project manager, and an accountant all at the same time.

Before any of this work begins, however, the IT consultant needs to determine the program's usefulness and practicality. This is also known as performing a feasibility study. Other key tasks include figuring out the cost of the proposed solution and planning how to make it work. The next task is to test the computer system, otherwise known as carrying out quality controls. Then the consultant teaches the employees how to use the new system and perform basic troubleshooting.

An IT consultant's work is broad based and varied, combining high-level technology skills with business know-how. IT consultants evaluate computer systems and perform technical work, such as installing new network servers. They also use their business skills to introduce the technology to senior management, explaining how the new servers will help the company increase profits and obtain more customers. As CNN reported in a 2018 blog post, "Everyone from local startups to the Fortune 500 companies needs IT consultants to help them figure out the cheapest and fastest ways to run computers."

Although every company needs IT consultants, it is helpful to specialize in a few select industries rather than trying to be all things to all people. This advice comes from IT consultant Steve Perkins, who began his career in government IT before transitioning to IT and management consulting for professional services firm Grant Thornton. "One of the first questions prospective clients are likely to ask is what kind of experience you have in their industry, so focusing on particular sectors and gaining lots of experience might help land assignments," he said in a 2018 article on the *CIO* website.

Regardless of what sector they specialize in, IT consultants usually juggle more than one project at a time, and they may need to shift their focus from one project to another in a single day. This is what makes consulting work challenging yet rewarding. According to a 2017 blog post on the IT job site Career Mash, "IT consultants are the ultimate problem solvers who juggle numerous tasks on any given day to help clients reduce costs, improve efficiency and make company tech more secure, effective and intuitive for all kinds of users."

Education

An associate's degree in computer science, information technology, or management information systems is sufficient for some IT consultants, although a bachelor's degree is preferred, according to the career website Monster. Workers who hold a master of science or a master of business administration (MBA) degree are at an advantage to earn higher-paying positions.

However, technology writer Jayne Thompson points out that experience can sometimes be more important than a formal degree. "The term 'information technology consultant' is not protected in the United States as a professional title, so there's no rule about having any type of degree or qualification," she wrote in a 2018 blog post on the tech site Chron. "The types of clients who hire consultants are more likely to care about the consultant's track record in delivering IT change programs than in his/her technical credentials." Nonetheless, aspiring IT consultants would be wise to obtain a bachelor's degree in software engineering, computer science, or a related field. They should then work as a database administrator or a network engineer for about three years. This experience will give them the background and credentials to strike out on their own.

Certification

IT consultants are expected to be experts in a wide variety of technical areas, such as network engineering, database administration, cloud computing, systems planning, and project management. For that reason, certification in information systems security, networking, and Scrum management can be valuable. Students can obtain information on these and other certifications from the websites of the organizations that offer them (Microsoft,

Cisco, and Scrum), or they can check out a number of online boot camps and tech schools. In some cases, prerequisites and IT work experience are required to become certified. "Most IT training companies offer instructor-led training (ILT) as well as online computer-based training (CBT) options," explained IT consultant Ed Tittel in a 2018 Business News Daily blog post. "Look for companies that provide the specific courses and certification training you need to develop new or deeper skills and knowledge in your chosen IT niche."

Volunteer Work and Internships

Because a career as an IT consultant typically requires at least three years of experience as, say, a database administrator or network engineer, it is not an entry-level position. For that reason, internships and volunteer opportunities with the specific title of IT consultant are rarely available. With that in mind, students majoring in computer science or information technology should aim for internships as computer systems analysts, sometimes called systems architects. These IT professionals study an organization's current computer systems and procedures and design ways to help them operate more efficiently and effectively.

Many technology companies offer paid and unpaid internships to college students with the possibility that they will be offered a full-time job after they graduate. Internships are also offered at large retail organizations, energy companies, insurance firms, health care organizations (hospital systems, medical device companies, and biotechnology firms), government agencies, and colleges and universities. To learn more about specific internships, students should check out the websites of the organizations that interest them. Internship listings can also be found on popular career websites such as Indeed, Simply Hired, Glassdoor, and Dice. "Any internship in IT will boost your résumé. Not only will internships help you apply your course skills, but you'll also learn how to interact with clients," advises the author of a 2018 post on Computer Science Degree Hub, an online resource for IT education. "The business communication skills you'll learn are as vital as your computer-related intern duties."

Skills and Personality

IT consultants need to possess a combination of strong technical skills, business knowledge, and good communication and presentation skills. Because they serve as lead project managers when clients want to expand their organization's computer network capabilities, they must understand various software and hardware components. Once a new system goes live, they need to stay onsite and debug any kinks or problems that may occur. They also need to train employees on how to navigate the new features.

Not all projects require the same types of tasks, and not all networks use the same operating system. That means IT consultants need to stay up to speed on technology developments and be able to "know it all" without projecting a "know-it-all" attitude. Most of all, they must gain the confidence and trust of their clients and work together as partners.

On the Job

Employers

Most IT consultants either work for large IT consulting firms and move from project to project or work for themselves and find their own clients. Major IT consulting firms include Deloitte, Booz Allen Hamilton, Gartner, Hewlett Packard Enterprise, IBM, Science Applications International Corporation, and others. Many enterprise software companies, such as Microsoft, employ their own IT consultants for services related to their products.

Working Conditions

IT consultants work indoors, often in corporate settings. Most work full-time, and overtime is often required. These long hours can pose a challenge, according to IT consultant Michael Schmid. "We are pretty much on call 24/7 for business-critical issues, so this type of work can be really demanding and stressful," he commented in an e-mail interview with the author. "When things go bad and you have a server down and the company is losing money by the minute until you get the server back online, you will feel the stress."

An IT consultant installs new network servers. Before this stage, she would have presented a report to company executives on the benefits of having the new servers.

Earnings

The Bureau of Labor Statistics (BLS) does not offer a specific category for IT consultants. The median 2018 salary for its closest related category, computer systems analysts, was $88,270 per year. According to Glassdoor, IT consultant annual salaries ranged from about $83,860 to $175,890.

Opportunities for Advancement

Entry-level IT consultants who work for large firms can get promoted to senior positions, which means they have more responsibilities, must frequently travel—often to places like London, Dublin, Paris, Hong Kong, and Singapore—and earn higher salaries. Occasionally, IT consultants advance to the level of chief information officer (CIO). This senior position is responsible for growing a company's business. For this reason, the CIO serves as a company's leading strategist, or big-picture thinker and planner, and determines which area of technology will be most important in the future. "The [CIO] position continues to change with the advances in technology," reported tech writer Laura Schneider in a September 2018 blog post on the Balance Careers website. The media salary for a CIO is $154,614, according to the BLS, and an MBA is recommended.

What Is the Future Outlook for Information Technology Consultants?

Although the BLS does not keep data specific to IT consultants, there will be approximately 115,200 more management consultancy jobs by 2026, according to the tech site Chron. This represents a 12 percent growth rate, which is higher than the average projected growth for other IT positions. The demand for consulting services of any type is expected to grow as companies seek ways to become more technologically efficient and control costs. In other words, the future is bright for IT consultants.

Find Out More

CompTIA Association of Information Technology Professionals (AITP)
3500 Lacey Rd., Suite 100
Downers Grove, IL 60515
website: www.aitp.org

The AITP is the leading association for technology professionals (including IT consultants), students, and educators. Members strengthen their professional network, improve their technical knowledge and business skills, develop a personal career path, and keep current on technology and business trends. The organization offers a special program for students called the CompTIA AITP Student Program, which connects students to mentors and provides career advice and resources to build a strong foundation as an IT professional.

IEEE Computer Society
10662 Los Vaqueros Cir.
Los Alamitos, CA 90720-1314
website: www.computer.org

Part of the Institute of Electrical and Electronics Engineers, the IEEE Computer Society is the world's leading membership organization dedicated to computer science and technology. Serving more than sixty thousand members, the society is a trusted source for information, networking, and career development. It serves a global community of technology leaders, including IT consultants. The organization sponsors more than two hundred technical conferences and events each year, including the industry-oriented Rock Stars series, aimed at research and industry professionals. In addition, the organization's publications are peer reviewed, indexed, and authored by technology thought leaders worldwide.

Network Professional Association (NPA)

3517 Camino del Rio S., Suite 215
San Diego, CA 92108-4098
website: www.npanet.org

The NPA is a self-regulating, nonprofit association of network computing professionals, including IT consultants, that sets standards of technical expertise and professionalism. Members participate in various boards, local chapters, committees, and councils. The NPA also offers membership to students who are enrolled in information technology classes at accredited colleges.

Women in Technology (WIT)

200 Little Falls St., Suite 205
Falls Church, VA 22046
website: www.womenintechnology.org

WIT is advancing women in technology, including women who serve as IT consultants, by providing advocacy, leadership, professional development, networking, mentoring, and technology education. Members work in government and in private industry, and they benefit from their interactions with others at all stages of their careers.

Interview with a Business Intelligence Analyst

Brian Green is a business intelligence analyst with Vistage World-wide, a San Diego–based membership organization that provides professional peer advisory services for executives. Green has worked as a business intelligence analyst for seven years. In an interview conducted via e-mail, he provided answers to the author's questions.

Q: Why did you become a business intelligence analyst?

A: This is a second career for me. In my first career, I saw that administrators made decisions more by personal observation than by scientific data. I was struck that there were many ways to learn about our customers' experiences, but these weren't used much. I also realized that when these tools were used, the data was locked away from key stakeholders because they were afraid of what the data might show. Would this information somehow embarrass them? I then became passionate about data and its possible uses.

Fortunately, my employer encouraged my career change. Since I already had a master's and a bachelor's degree, I did not need more formal education. Instead, I took coding and other technical classes and created a new position at my company as a data analyst. After three years, I was promoted to business intelligence analyst. Six months later, I found a great new opportunity at Vistage!

I've learned that working in data means understanding people's needs as well as code syntax. If I do my job well, it means someone at my company can make a key decision and have data to support it. My passion is not in the writing of the code or the building of a dashboard. Rather, it's using data or information to help my employer, Vistage, to learn which consulting services would help its executive clients the most. Once I obtain the raw data—or information from surveys and questionnaires that we give to our executive customers—I can prepare a report that shows what these executives are concerned about the most. Maybe it's high employee turnover, or maybe it's losing market share to a competitor. Then our management team can decide what services to offer our clients.

Q: Can you describe your typical workday?

A: My day starts by checking my e-mail. If there is an emergency request, I respond to it quickly. Much of my day is spent working alone on requests or communicating with business stakeholders about what type of data they are interested in reviewing. Before any code is written, I need to be clear on what the business really needs, and the decision makers must agree on what they need. Once they communicate the "why," I may have a helpful suggestion for the business. It is also possible that the solution they are seeking has already been built and can be leveraged to solve their current problem.

Once I'm clear on what the business needs, I can begin coding. My company uses SQL, which stands for structured query language. SQL allows me to write a series of commands that will extract the exact data that I need. If the end users want their data in a more visual format, I'll take the output of the code I've written and connect it to Tableau, a data visualization tool. In Tableau, I can create charts and graphs to illustrate relationships in the data. By adding filters, I can help the business users engage with their data as well as help them ask more questions.

Q: What do you like most about your job?

A: There are few times I've ever experienced boredom at work. There is always a new challenge to learn from. I like that through research I can find the answer for myself. I also like that I can spend half my day with headphones on not talking with anyone and the other half engaging the business about the data. It makes my day diverse and engaging. It's gratifying when you are trying to solve an issue for a data request and you realize what the solution is.

Q: What do you like least about your job?
A: It's difficult after spending hours on a data request and later finding out the business user didn't really do anything with the data output I provided. Maybe a more important project has come up, and the business user needs to focus on that new project instead. Maybe he or she has simply decided this data is not necessary right now and the information is temporarily put aside. In business, priorities shift a lot, and what may seem vital on a Monday may not be so pressing by Friday.

Q: What personal qualities do you find most valuable for this type of work?
A: An analyst must be curious because he or she will spend a lot of time asking questions about why a thing is occurring. For example, if you get an error message from your code, you have to want to understand why that happened. Also, attention to detail is critical because if a single element in a line of code is incorrect, it will render your entire result inaccurate. An analyst must also be tenacious because a request may be unclear or a solution may be difficult, but throwing up your hands is not an option; in fact, it is surmounting these challenges that makes the job so enjoyable.

Q: What is the best way to prepare for this type of job?
A: There are so many online programs and resources that someone interested in this type of work should invest time in learning: SQL, Tableau, Excel, PowerBI, R, SSIS, SSRS, and Python. There is so much content on YouTube along with web resources like W3Schools and others. An internship would be a strong avenue for gaining the necessary skills, experience, and perspective to successfully move forward. Lastly, it is critically important to be persistent and realize that there is no one way to pursue a career in data.

Other Jobs in Information Technology

Cloud engineer
Computer and information research scientist
Computer and information systems manager
Computer, ATM, and office machine repairer
Computer forensic investigator
Computer network architect
Computer programmer
Computer systems administrator
Computer systems analyst
Computer vision engineer
Data engineer
Data scientist
DevOps engineer
DevOps lead
Electrical engineer
Front-end engineer
Hardware engineer
Health IT specialist

Information security analyst
Information technology vendor manager
IOT (Internet of Things) designer
Machine learning engineer
Management analyst
Market research analyst
Multimedia artist and animator
Network analyst
Network architect
Product manager
Quality assurance engineer
Security analyst
Security management specialist
Site reliability engineer
Software applications developer
Software engineer
User-support specialist

Editor's note: The US Department of Labor's Bureau of Labor Statistic provides information about hundreds of occupations. The agency's *Occupational Outlook Handbook* describes what these jobs entail, the work environment, education and skill requirements, pay, future outlook, and more. The *Occupational Outlook Handbook* may be accessed online at www.bls.gov/ooh.

Index

Note: Boldface page numbers indicate illustrations.